The Library of Author Biographies™

Karen Hesse

The Library of Author Biographies™

KAREN HESSE

Nzingha Clarke

rosen
central™

The Rosen Publishing Group, Inc., New York

Published in 2006 by The Rosen Publishing Group, Inc.
29 East 21st Street, New York, NY 10010

Library of Congress Cataloging-in-Publication

Clarke, Nzingha.
Karen Hesse/Nzingha Clarke.
    p. cm.—(The library of author biographies)
Includes bibliographical references and index.
ISBN 1-4042-0462-8 (library binding)
1. Hesse, Karen. 2. Authors, American—20th century—Biography.
I. Title. II. Series.
PS3558.E797867Z64 2006
813'.6—dc22

                                                                2004027882

Manufactured in the United States of America

From "Newbery Winner Adds Somber Voice to Revised Summer Reading Lists," June 30, 1998. © The Associated Press. All rights reserved. Reprinted with permission.
From AUTHORS AND ARTISTS FOR YOUNG ADULTS, by Gale Group, © 2003, Gale Group. Reprinted by permission of The Gale Group.
From SOMETHING ABOUT THE AUTHOR AUTOBIOGRAPHY SERIES, by Gale Group, © 2000, Gale Group. Reprinted by permission of The Gale Group.
From WRITERS FOR YOUNG ADULTS, by Lois T. Stover, Gale Group, © 2000, Gale Group. Reprinted by permission of The Gale Group.
From *Book Links*, September 1999. Copyright © American Library Association. Used with permission.
From *The Horn Book Magazine*, July/August 1998. Reprinted by permission of The Horn Book, Inc., Boston, MA, www.hbook.com.
From Eighth Book of Juniors Authors and Illustrators, Copyright © 2000, edit by Connie c. Rockman. Reprinted with permission of The H. W. Wilson Company
Quotes from Hendershot, Judith, & Peck, Jacqueline. (1999, May). Newberry Medal winner Karen Hesse brings Billie Jo's voice Out of the Dust. *The Reading Teacher*, 52(8), 856-858. Reprinted with permission of the International Reading Association.
From Ellen Bryant. "Honoring the Complexities of Our Lives: An Interview with Karen Hesse." *Voices from the Middle.* Copyright 1997 by the National Council of Teachers of English. Reprinted with permission.
From Cathy Beck, and Linda Gwyn, Dick Koblitz, Anne O'Connor, Kathryn Mitchell Pierce, Susan Wolf. "Talking About Books: Karen Hesse." *Language Arts.* Copyright 1999 by the National Council of Teachers of English. Reprinted with permission.

Table of Contents

Introduction: An Accidental Writer

Karen Hesse did not start out with the goal of changing the face of young adult literature. As much as she has always loved stories and storytelling, she did not even start out with the ambition of becoming a writer. And yet, she has written eighteen books so far, and that includes four picture books for younger readers.

"I write the kinds of books that I would have wanted when I was a child,"[1] Hesse explains. When she was young, Hesse's life was difficult. She was very shy and not often comfortable in her environment. In books she found other worlds and other lives to live in. She escaped into the stories she read, and as her own imagination grew, she became a storyteller capable of dazzling her friends with the tales she made up to share with them.

Today, Karen Hesse's writing is changing the landscape of young adult books. Her first book, *Wish on a Unicorn* (1991), takes place in the present day. Yet most of her books take us back to another era to investigate a world very different from the one we now live in. In historical settings, Hesse tells the story of characters she has created. Hesse puts an enormous amount of energy into research and telling an accurate story in her historical fiction books. Her commitment has made her one of the best writers of the genre for young adults. For example, *Out of the Dust* (1997) is the story about Billie Jo Kelby's life during the Depression's Dust Bowl days—a time of drought when dust blew hundreds of miles across the Great Plains and killed crops and people. Hesse's editor Brenda Bowen remarked that Hesse's depiction of the dryness of the land and the dust in the air was so complete that readers cough as if they were experiencing these conditions themselves.

"The reason I'm drawn to historical fiction can be pegged to the fact that the past often resonates in the present in a compelling way," Hesse says. "The advantage to writing about the past is that one can employ an objective historical perspective, rather than having to sort through the chaos of emotions when one is living through an event. If readers derive from my book nothing more than a good read, I'm happy. If readers find echoes of the past stretching forward to deepen their understanding and compassion for the victims of contemporary struggles, I am equally pleased. My hope is simply that I have created something worthy of the reader's precious time."[2]

In all of Hesse's books, whether she is writing about a Vermont town trying to face down the racism of the Ku Klux Klan (*Witness*, 2001) or about a teenager as she deals with the aftermath of a nuclear disaster (*Phoenix Rising*, 1994), Hesse is committed to asking the hard, unanswerable questions. The subject and circumstances Hesse chooses are not easy or comfortable, but her readers love her books for their depth of emotion and the way she uses language to make her readers feel what her characters feel. One could say that her gift is the ability to get near the reader's heart and teach it something new. Maybe it is a new way of thinking. Maybe it is a new way of looking at the world.

The characters in Hesse's novels often find themselves in situations in which it is not clear what they should do. Usually, they know what they want, but they are youths in a world of adults, and they do not have the power to make what they want happen. So they must be smart and resourceful and pay close attention to the world around them.

In telling her characters' stories, honesty is the most important thing to Hesse. "I never consider telling anything less than the truth in the books I write," she says. "It is irresponsible and disrespectful to my readers to sugarcoat life, to leave out the pain . . . Young readers are bright and perceptive, and they can spot a dishonest depiction or a half-truth a mile away. I wouldn't insult them or waste their time with a less than honest portrayal of a time and place and people."[3] Whether her character is trying to take care of her younger sister and brother in the midst of poverty and being bullied, like Mags does in *Wish on a Unicorn*, or misses the family of dolphins that raised her, like Mila in *The Music of Dolphins* (1996), Hesse's vision of her characters' lives is clear and true. It is as if her reader is standing in Mags's shoes, or Mila's shoes, eager to know what will happen next.

Hesse once stated, "I never do anything in halves,"[4] and when you look at the life she's led, it is clear that that is an understatement. As we will see in the following chapters, hers is a rare level of commitment—to ideas, people, projects, and life. This commitment is clearly evident in her writing. Hesse is a complete storyteller, and the stories she tells engage her readers as completely as she is engaged when she writes.

"The feeling I get when I write is akin to dropping through a trap door into the flow of an underground river," Hesse says. "I stand in the current and just as a plant absorbs nutrients and energy from its surroundings, I absorb the energy of this subterranean river through my soul. This is not willed, it simply happens."[5]

It may seem hard to believe that Hesse did not come directly to writing as a profession. At one time she wanted to be an actress. As a child she dreamed of being an ambassador and an archaeologist. Later she studied anthropology and psychology, but it seems that ultimately, writing has given Hesse a way to be all the things she once dreamed of being. About Karen Hesse as an actress, Bowen, who has edited seven of Hesse's books, says, "The thing[s] I know for sure about Karen Hesse [are]: as quiet as she appears, she is a born performer, and once she's on stage—whether on a panel at IRA [International Reading Association], or in a cafeteria crowded with 150 Long Island fifth graders—she shines."[6] Writing allows Hesse to be an actress in a different guise. As a researcher, Hesse is uncovering the bones of history, just as the archaeologist she dreamed of being would. She is an ambassador, explaining and bringing an understanding of history and of other generations to her readers. The worlds she describes may have existed hundreds of years ago, or their existence may be as recent as our parents' and our grandparents' childhoods. As an ambassador between then and now, Hesse may give us insight into the history of our families, or simply, another angle from which to look at the world. At the beginning of her life, Karen Hesse pointed herself in one direction and it was surprising when writing accidentally captured her attention. But this happy accident has been to the benefit of readers of all ages.

1 West Garrison Avenue

Karen Hesse was born in Baltimore, Maryland, on August 29, 1952, to Frances Broth and Alvin Donald. From the moment of her birth she was a sickly child, almost starving to death because her stomach could not digest baby formula. Looking for a way to treat her underdevelopment, a pediatrician realized that Karen could probably digest goat's milk. Finally, she began to grow. Still, her childhood was marked by illness after illness and she describes herself as having been an extremely whiny child. In fact, she was so unhappy that her mother offered a gold star for each day Karen got through without crying. As much as she loved the idea of earning the gold stars, she never managed to collect many.

Karen's father worked as a collection man. Before there were credit cards, which allow people to borrow money from the card company as long as they pay back the money they spent, people—poor people, particularly—used to buy what they needed for their homes from stores that allowed them to pay a little each week for their purchases. Karen's father's job was to collect money each week at the homes of the people who owed his boss for the furniture and appliances he had sold to them.

Sometimes Karen would ride the unpaved back roads of Maryland with her father as he did his job. She saw "the tarpaper shacks sheltering several generations of a family under one roof,"[1] and she realized that while her family may have struggled financially, their lives were much more comfortable than the lives of the people on her father's collection route. This experience, and seeing the respect with which Karen's father treated the people from whom he collected, was an important lesson for Karen. When describing her first book, *Wish on a Unicorn*, she stated, "I remembered the humor and dignity of the individuals on my father's collection route and I tried settling some of that dignity on the shoulders of my protagonist, Mags."[2]

When Karen started school, her mother went to work part-time as a substitute teacher at Hesse's school. Later, when Karen began first grade, her mother found full-time work as the receptionist at a beauty parlor.

Childhood Friendships

Karen grew up on West Garrison Avenue in the Pimlico section of Baltimore. Pimlico was a crowded city neighborhood, filled with small row houses and plenty of other children with whom to play. After school and in the summers, all the neighborhood kids played together, sometimes putting on talent shows for the neighborhood, or just having fun and finding trouble to get into.

Karen's fragile health as a child did not keep her from joining the fun or having adventures. When Karen was about eight years old, one of her best friends was a boy named Stuart who lived across the alley from Karen. One time, Karen was convinced that she could fly. Stuart challenged her to prove it, and she obliged! She stood at the top of the second floor inside her house and flew over the steps. She hit the last step with a thud so loud her mother came to see what had happened.

When Stuart continued to doubt her abilities, Karen, encouraged by her first attempt at flight, was eager to try flying from the second floor window of her bedroom. Luckily, Stuart's mother spotted Karen sitting on her window ledge, preparing to fly. Stuart's mother phoned Karen's mother, who managed to grab Karen just moments before her big jump.

Joey was another friend on Karen's block. Because Joey's hearing was impaired, he wore a large, old-fashioned hearing aid. The boys in the neighborhood tended not to include him in their games. Joey was two years older than Karen, and that meant that with Joey, Karen was allowed to cross streets that she was not allowed to cross alone. Although they couldn't easily communicate due to his hearing impairment, they could share experiences like walking to Cylburn Park to enjoy a taste of nature in the middle of the city. Hesse's story *Lester's Dog* (1993) is based on her childhood friendship with Joey.

The Quiet Observer

Though there was no shortage of friends to play with, Karen spent much of her time alone. The house Karen grew up in felt cramped, and her parents fought with each other a lot. Sickly and painfully shy, Karen dealt with the unhappiness of her home by living in her imagination and losing herself in the world of books. Rather than go home after school, Karen spent hours swinging on swings in the schoolyard. At home, Karen found peace and quiet by climbing the apple tree in the backyard of her house with a book and reading in the tree for hours.

About her childhood, Hesse says, "I'm not certain when I realized I wasn't like my friends. But from an early age it felt right to keep my inner world a secret. As a result people thought of me as shy; I was an observer of life more than a full-fledged participant."[3] And though Karen felt that people tended to ignore her, she was keenly aware of her environment.

Protectors and Role Models

Many of the main characters in Hesse's books are girls who are taken care of and protected by adults other than their parents. In Hesse's own childhood, her life was positively affected by the community of adults around her who helped her in a variety of ways. "My extended family filled in quite a few gaps in the loose weave of my childhood," she says. "Beyond blood ties, people in my community—teachers, a librarian, neighbors—

took an interest and made me feel supported and treasured. And beyond them, my literary family, books, characters, kept me afloat during the times I was too tired to keep dog-paddling in the rapids of my life."[4]

Hesse was very close to her maternal grandparents. Her grandfather had almost been a passenger on the *Titanic*, but he sold his ticket at the last minute and made the crossing on the next ship. One of Hesse's first memories is of watching her grandfather, an Orthodox Jew, as he prayed. Although Hesse never received a formal religious education, she was often at her grandparents' home, and from them she learned the traditions of the Jewish faith. Both *Poppy's Chair* (1993) and *Letters from Rifka* (1992) are inspired by Hesse's grandparents. Jewish culture plays a large role in many of Hesse's books (*Letters from Rifka*; *A Time of Angels* (1995); *The Stone Lamp: Eight Stories of Hanukkah Through History* (2003); and *The Cats in Kransinski Square* (2004)).

Her aunts Esther and Bern (short for Bernice) were also protectors and role models. In her Aunt Esther, Karen saw strength and responsibility that she admired and would later recall when she created the character of Hannah in *A Time of Angels*. Karen described her aunt Bern as cool, creative, and fun. Bern was both a friend and an inspiration to Karen as she was growing up. The experience of meeting (and being sorely disappointed by the arrival of) Bern's newborn daughter Lisa when Hesse was a child is recounted by her in the book *Lavender* (1993).

The attention and care of her grandparents and her aunts was a huge source of comfort for Karen growing up. She says, "I could be weepy, I could be cranky, I could say nothing and they loved me. I felt their unconditional love whenever I was with them. I am sure that at times my aunt and my grandparents wanted to tear their hair out because I was not easy to be with, but I never felt it. I always felt that they loved me no matter what I did."[5]

Relatives were not the only people who looked out for Karen. Because she was often ill and both her parents worked, Karen would go to the home of her neighbors, the Somellas, when she was sent home sick from school. The Somellas had a son, Charlsey, who was much older than Karen. It was Charlsey's grandmother Bubbi Hannah with whom Karen spent her time. She took care of Karen on the days Karen could not be at school. A few years ago, a young reader, whose name is also Hannah, pointed out to Hesse that she has often used the name Hannah for characters in her books. Hesse hadn't noticed this pattern, but she remembers Bubbi Hannah so fondly from her childhood that it seems likely she was unconsciously celebrating her childhood caretaker.

From believing that she could fly to reading in a tree, Karen's imagination and her love of books was fed by Peggy Coughlin, the librarian at Enoch Pratt Free Library, in Karen's neighborhood. Karen was a voracious reader, even reading by moonlight or the light from streetlamps, long after her parents thought she was asleep at night. Dr. Seuss was Karen's first favorite author because she loved his use of language and the moral lessons of his books. *Horton Hatches the Egg* was one of Karen's favorite books as a child. Peggy Coughlin stoked the fire of Karen's love for words with the books she suggested. Even though she has never written the sort of rhyming poetry that Dr. Seuss wrote, she feels that the "music of his language"[6] and the way he played with words was the first inspiration for her poetry.

Discovering New Talents

Karen was shy and willing to fade into the background for the sake of observing the world around her. However, Karen's life began to take a turn when a series of teachers and events made her and the people around her aware of her talents.

In fourth grade, Karen's teacher Mrs. Sugar volunteered Karen to teach English after school at the home of a new classmate whose family had just emigrated from Israel. Karen had no interest in teaching Mickey Czarney, a girl who looked enough like Karen that they might have been each other's double. But she did as she was told. Each day after school, she went home with Mickey to read to Mickey and her family. She taught them the English words for the objects around them, and she talked to them. Soon the whole family was speaking English, and they all spoke just like Karen! She and Mickey became best friends. The strength of spirit in Rifka, the main character in *Letters from Rifka*, is based on Karen's observations of Mickey Czarney.

In fifth grade, Karen's life was forever changed when her teacher Mrs. Datnoff marked a story Karen had written about a bubble world with a big check and the note "Very Creative." She says, "I was this kid who did not have a lot of positive reinforcement, so to have this 'Very Creative' was a gift to me. From that point on, I believed myself to be very creative. In spite of years of rejection, I always played that little tape in my head. It was a fifth-grade teacher who gave me the gift of believing in myself."[7]

As Karen commenced to value her creativity, her imagination flourished. She began writing poetry and started to think of herself as a writer. In her words, "Finally I had an outlet. I'd been holding so much in, and I couldn't say the real things, but I could begin to address the feeling of isolation that I felt then, that any adolescent feels."[8] Her workspace was the closet of her bedroom, where she sat and wrote her heart and soul into notebook after notebook. Years later, some of this work would be published and win awards.

By sixth grade, Karen was confident in her abilities as a writer. Her teacher Clifton Ball recognized and praised her creativity and talent. Although she was still so shy that she couldn't bear to look people in the eye, she rose to the task when Mr. Ball asked her to write the speech for the sixth-grade graduation. She did, but she hadn't expected to be asked to read the speech she had written! Mr. Ball had complete confidence that she could speak in front of a crowd. The auditorium was packed when the usually tongue-tied Karen stood up to address her fellow students, their parents, and teachers. She delivered her speech with a poise that surprised her and everyone, except Mr. Ball. It was a big moment in Karen's life. It changed her view of herself, and it even changed the way her mother saw her. She says, "My mom had never really seen me before that day."[9]

2 Hiding in Stories

Hesse is not particularly forthright in publicly discussing her childhood or personal life. Often in autobiographical statements, she has been (perhaps purposefully) vague. In researching her life, it is not uncommon to find that important details are missing; that an important event is referred to but never explained; or, that the timing of a circumstance is unclear. Between the lines of what is said, it seems evident that perhaps twice as much has not been said.

Even her editor Brenda Bowen has commented that after fifteen years of friendship and working together, she does not know much about Hesse either. Hesse has an older brother named Mark with whom she was very close when they were children. Hesse's brother fought for a time in the Vietnam War (1965–1975). Hesse says very little about her parents (the least is said about her mother, and what is said suggests a difficult relationship). In various interviews and accounts of Hesse's life, it becomes evident that her parents divorced. The people she now refers to as her father and sister are actually her stepfather and stepsister. Although her mother remarried in 1968, it seems that her stepfather had been a family friend of long standing. Also, it seems that Hesse had grown up considering her sister as one of her best friends, long before the two became family.

The Angels at Midnight

The most revealing work of Hesse's is the autobiographical story "Waiting for Midnight" that she contributed to the book *When I Was Your Age, Volume Two* (1999). In this story, she tells what it felt like to live in a family in which her parents fought all the time. Karen is about eleven years old in the story. At eleven, her mother was sick (Hesse doesn't say what the illness was) and had almost died—twice. Karen was made responsible for preparing her mother's food. She worried about her mother's health, all while she herself was often sick.

She didn't feel she could talk to anyone about her parents or how afraid she was that her mother might die. And there was also another difficult situation Karen did not feel she could discuss: the children next door.

Next door to Karen's family lived a woman who had had a nervous breakdown. The woman was mentally ill, and she scared Karen. When she talked to Karen, Karen ran away as quickly as she could. The woman was strange to talk to, but the big secret was the way she treated her children. Karen's neighbor had two children, a girl and a boy who were older than Karen.

In "Waiting for Midnight," Karen writes that each night, as she tried to sleep, the woman next door locked her children in the closet for the night. The small row house where Karen lived was the mirror image of the house next door, and her closet shared a wall with the closet of her neighbors. Through the wall she could hear as the daughter and son pleaded with their mother to be let out of the closet. Her neighbor's cruelty to her children scared Karen. The begging voices of the kids next door kept her awake. Bubbi Hannah's family lived two doors down from Karen, on the other side of the crazy neighbor's house. Yet when she spent the afternoons with Bubbi Hannah, Karen was afraid to ask if Bubbi Hannah knew about the ways their neighbor abused her children.

Karen's nights were filled with fear as she lay in bed listening to the voices of the children next door and to the sounds of her parents fighting. To survive the nights, she read and she daydreamed. Reading helped her to ignore her neighbors' voices. She would often read by flashlight so as not to alert her parents that she was still up. Another way Karen spent these nights was by making up fabulous stories for the talent shows that the kids in her neighborhood held. These stories would keep her friends on the edge of their seats when she told them the next day.

"At night I would fantasize that I was an ambassador between [Soviet premier Nikita] Khrushchev and [United States president John F.] Kennedy," she remembers. "I would be the person who would save the world because I would make these two people understand each other and resolve their differences . . . that's when I discovered the power of fiction because it was very comforting for me to feel as if I had some control and I could do something, and that's what creating fiction is all about."[1]

A favorite book of Karen's was a collection of stories about K'Tonton, a Jewish Tom Thumb–type character. One story took place during Shavous, a Jewish holiday. In the story, K'Tonton planned to make a wish at midnight for something he wanted. In the end, however, K'Tonton uses his midnight wish to help someone else. Remembering the story of K'Tonton, Karen decided that when Shavous came, she would stay up until midnight to ask God for help. There was plenty that needed fixing. She could ask for help for herself and her family. She could also make a wish on behalf of the children next door. It wasn't easy to stay up so late, but on the night of Shavous, she managed to stay awake. However, just as midnight struck, Karen describes seeing angels, real angels, entering our atmosphere from the sky. She held her breath and watched. She stared at the beauty of it, and she forgot to make her wishes. In "Waiting for Midnight," Karen explains that she was disappointed to realize that she had missed her opportunity. However, shortly after this night—miraculously and mysteriously— the police came and removed the children from the house next door.

This would not be the only time Hesse would see spirits from the other world. As an adult, she and her husband lived in a house with the ghost of the house's former owner! According to Hesse, this ghost was friendly and helpful and it liked Hesse and her husband. In fact, it liked them so much that when they started looking for a new place to live, every opportunity fell through until Hesse explained to the ghost why she felt they needed to move. After her explanation, everything went smoothly, and Hesse and her husband were able to move to their new house with the ghost's blessing.

A Changing World

The appearance of the angels at Shavous helped give Hesse a little hope, but the events of the world kept her serious and anxious. Having fantasized her place in the world as the mediator between Soviet premier Nikita Khrushchev (1894–1971) and U.S. president John F. Kennedy (1917–1963), Karen was devastated when the president was assassinated on November 22, 1963. When the announcement was made at her school, all the children were sent home. The nation was in mourning. Karen took his death so hard that after watching the president's funeral on television, she began folding everything, from towels to clothes, into a tight triangle the way she had seen the flag folded before it was handed to Jacqueline Kennedy, the president's widow.

By the time she was twelve years old, Karen had read most of the books in the children's section of the Enoch Pratt Free Library. She began to sneak over to the adults' section when she thought she could get away with it. In the adults' section, Karen found the book *Hiroshima*, by John Hersey. *Hiroshima* is a famous and classic book based on Hersey's interviews with six ordinary residents of the city of Hiroshima, Japan, who survived the day the United States dropped the first atomic bomb. The bomb was dropped on the city on August 6, 1945, bringing about the end to World War II (1939–1945). The atomic bomb created more devastation in minutes than the world had ever seen. When Karen read Hersey's book, it changed the way she viewed the world. She later expressed some of her feelings about the scale of the human tragedy in such a situation when she wrote her book *Phoenix Rising*. But back then, when Karen was twelve years old and rereading *Hiroshima* over and over again, she knew her life had changed. "My childhood ended with the reading of that book,"[2] she says.

3 Growing Up

When Karen was fourteen years old, her family moved from their house on West Garrison Avenue to an apartment in another part of Baltimore. As a result of the move, Hesse and her brother had to give up their dog and all the privileges of living in a house (such as slamming doors and making noise). Nevertheless, Karen made new friends at school and in her neighborhood.

Taking to the Stage

When Karen was sixteen, she started acting because she was jealous of all the attention her stepsister, Randy, received. Randy and Karen were the same age. Randy was a talented dancer who, at sixteen, was already dancing professionally. In response, Karen began her life as an actress.

Karen immediately loved Joan Maruskin, the drama teacher at her high school. She also loved being onstage. She would disappear into a character so fully that she would be surprised to "wake up" and see her classmates crying from the strength of her performance.

This was a time of contradictions for Karen. On one hand, she was so nervous that she could not learn to drive. At Karen's school, all high school seniors took a drivers' education course in order to get their driver's license. When Karen took the course, she did well on all the tests she took in the classroom. However, each time she got behind the wheel of the car for driving practice, she was so nervous she nearly caused accidents everywhere she went. She failed her driving test and didn't learn to drive until she was much older. And yet, Karen was not nervous about performing. She loved it so much that whenever she was given the opportunity, she happily took the stage. When she went to watch her sister, Randy, dance on the *Kirby Scott Show* and one of the go-go dancers didn't show up, Karen even danced on a raised platform for a television audience.

In school, Karen was known for taking her acting very seriously. So, during her senior year, she decided to do something completely different when Pikesville Senior High had its yearly variety show. In contrast to her image as a dramatic actress, Karen learned a funny song called "Loving You Has Made Me Bananas" from her mother and performed it with a squeaky Brooklyn accent. She wore a brightly colored costume in the style of Carmen Miranda—a popular 1940s performer who originally sang the song and danced in a fruit-filled hat. She was a hit! The crowd went wild to see this new, different side of Karen. She credits this moment as the birth of her sense of humor.

During her last two years in high school, Karen shone as a performer and as a student. But all her good work was not enough to make up for the awful academic year she had had during tenth grade. At that time, the problems of her home life had been so bad that she had failed her math and French classes. She applied to colleges with the intention of studying acting and becoming a professional actress, but the schools she applied to did not accept her. Joan Maruskin saved the day. Maruskin introduced Karen to the theater department at Towson State College and campaigned on Karen's behalf. Through

Maruskin's persistence, Karen was finally accepted into the drama department.

Discovering New Loves

Karen started college in 1969. Her family did not have enough money to pay for her education, so Karen worked and tried to spend as little money as possible. As a freshman, Karen rented a room in the home of an elderly woman. She was so poor that her food allowance only allowed for one sandwich each day. She would divide the sandwich in half and have one half for lunch and the other half for dinner.

During Karen's freshman year at Towson, she met the other important Randy in her life. A mutual friend introduced her to Randy Hesse. It was love at first sight for both Karen and Randy. Randy's and Karen's backgrounds were very different. Karen came from a working-class Jewish neighborhood. Randy also grew up in Baltimore, but in an upper-class neighborhood. According to Karen, no one there "had ever met a Jewish girl before."[1]

After Karen met Randy, she decided to give up acting. For her, both theater and love required all of her energy and attention. She felt she had to make a choice, so she chose Randy. Neither

Karen's nor Randy's families approved of the relationship, but on Thanksgiving Day in 1971, Karen and Randy eloped.

During this period, America was at war in Vietnam and young men were being drafted to fight the war. Randy Hesse enlisted and was assigned to serve in the navy. He sailed from Norfolk, Virginia. The two married in hopes that Karen would be able to travel with Randy if he was shipped overseas. Karen quit school and moved to Norfolk. She lived in "a tiny apartment, in a volatile neighborhood, as Randy's ship would sail for a week, come back for a month, leave for a week." About that period of her life, she says, "The threat of Vietnam hung over our heads. I did a lot of growing during those years. That work is certainly reflected in my work today."[2]

When Randy's tour of duty with the navy ended, he and Karen moved back to College Park and both enrolled at the University of Maryland.

At school, Karen majored in English but also took a double minor in psychology and anthropology. Karen's lifelong love of reading was served with her new job at the university's library. She was able to get a work-study position in which the school gave her money for school in exchange for the time she spent working. Some of the students who became Hesse's best friends were her fellow student workers at the library.

Karen loved being back in school. Moreover, she loved being part of the university's English department. Her studies and the friends she made there were a perfect fit. It was an environment of ideas and creative exploration, and Karen thrived. She applied herself seriously to writing poetry. By the time she graduated, she was already beginning to enjoy success as a poet. Her work was being published, she read her poetry to appreciative audiences, and she received invitations to present her poetry on other college campuses.

Karen graduated from college in 1975 and worked for one year at the University of Maryland as a leave-benefits coordinator, while her husband, Randy, finished his studies.

The year 1976 marked America's 200th birthday as a free and independent country. Karen and Randy Hesse joined the country's celebration of its bicentennial year by exploring the country after Randy graduated. They had a pickup truck, two cats, one tent, and camping supplies. For six months they drove, camped, and explored the country. All over the country, at campsites and in towns, they met and talked to people. They did not know where they might settle down, but when they arrived in Brattleboro, Vermont, they fell in love with it. Karen says, "I knew as soon as we crossed the Connecticut River from New Hampshire into Vermont that I'd come home."[3]

4 Becoming a Mother Changes Everything

In their new home in Vermont, Hesse continued to write poetry. Having loved working in a library during her school years, she always tried to find work that allowed her to keep reading and thinking about words.

Hesse became pregnant with her first child in 1978. It was a happy occasion, but very suddenly she stopped being able to write poetry. "My body and brain were at that point creating life, and so the creative energy seemed to channel inward rather than outward. What I wrote had no integrity to it," she says. She was frustrated by the change. "I couldn't block off enough creative energy to write in the way I had always written, with that same total focus,"[1] she says.

She wanted to write, and she felt that she needed to write. But it wasn't clear how she might find her writer's voice again if she wasn't going to write poetry. In preparation for the child she was carrying, Hesse began visiting the children's section of the library to read children's books. The sort of books that were offered to kids had changed a lot since Hesse's childhood days spent at the Enoch Pratt Free Library, and she was excited by the change. A librarian suggested she read *Of Nightingales That Weep*, by Katherine Paterson. She loved it! She says, "I read that book, and I thought if this is what children's literature is about, I want a part of it. I want a part of it so badly I can taste it."[2]

She went on to read everything that Paterson wrote. In Paterson's work, Hesse says she found " . . . an honesty and an integrity to her [Paterson's] work that made me so in awe that I thought . . . this is the best. It can't get any better that this. I want to do this."[3] For Hesse, Paterson's work marked the standard of writing she wanted to achieve in her own work. Whenever she had the opportunity, she went to hear the author speak, as well. She considered Paterson a mentor as she studied the craft of writing prose and writing for children.

It's a Writer's Life

Hesse and Randy Hesse's first child, Kate, was born in April 1979. By the time Kate arrived, Hesse was already committed to learning how to write for children. Hesse worked from home, fitting in her responsibilities as a freelance proofreader or as a typesetter for book compositors while Kate napped. Hesse put herself to bed once she'd settled her daughter to sleep for the night, but then woke up at 1 or 2 AM to write until Kate woke up, at around 7 AM. It was an exhausting schedule. Hesse says, "I'm sure I was cranky. I was certainly sleep deprived. But I'm crankier still when I don't write!"[4] Hesse continued to write, and she continued this grueling schedule after her second child, Rachel, was born in May 1982.

For years, Hesse wrote book after book for children and young adults without realizing any of the success or acknowledgment she had known as a poet. She continued to study the novels of other writers she admired. She joined a writing group that would be instrumental in helping to improve and refine her talents as a writer. She began sending her work to publishers in 1985, but everything she wrote was rejected.

Another writer might have given up, but Hesse's commitment to her chosen path was absolute. Her first editor recognized this dedication and talent. The first story Brenda Bowen ever read by Hesse was about a family's encounter with Bigfoot. She didn't like the plot or the story. However, she did respond to the strength of Hesse's writing, especially her sense of place. She saw the extraordinary talent Hesse has for making her readers see and feel the locations of her stories. She knew that Hesse was a good writer, but at that time the stories she was telling weren't working.

New Inspiration

Hesse continued to write and when a situation arose that had a life-changing effect on her, the way she approached her writing improved as a result. Hesse's grandmother, to whom she was quite close, had become sick and was dying of cancer. As her illness went into its final stages, she was cared for by hospice volunteers at her aunt Bern's home. Hesse was impressed by these hospice volunteers, whose presence allowed her grandmother to die peacefully. Inspired by the volunteers' commitment to hospice care, Hesse decided to become a hospice volunteer, as well. The volunteer training changed her life. She says, "Hospice training forced me to look at myself, at my own mortality. It was that kind of reckoning that enabled me to be so honest in my work."[5]

As her relationship to herself and her own life changed, she began to see her work in a different way. She had been writing stories in the fantasy genre and though she was writing about the same issues that continue to interest her— namely, separation and loss—she says, "I just wasn't dealing with them in a fully realized way. When I took the hospice training, I had to look at myself all the way to the core. It made me think and respond on a level that I never had before. Because I was denying so much of who I was, because I had not confronted so much of who I was, how could I confront it in my work? Once I was able to look at my whole self, I could then perhaps create a whole, believable fictional world and characters who had solidity and substance and credibility."[6]

Following hospice training and the deepening effect it had on her writing, Hesse sent another story she had written to Bowen. It was years later, but Bowen remembered Hesse's earlier story. The new story was called *Wish on a Unicorn*. It was only six pages long. Hesse had written the story to be a picture book for young children. Again, Bowen liked the writing, but didn't like the plot. And it was too short to really explore the lives of the interesting characters Hesse had created. She asked Hesse to expand the story. Hesse's next draft was forty pages. But Bowen still didn't like the plot. When Hesse expanded the story further, turning in a 106-page manuscript, Bowen was finally satisfied. *Wish on a Unicorn* was the first of Hesse's books to be published. Hesse had spent almost nine long years submitting her writing to publishers before her first book was accepted for publication. About the hard years before publishing her first book, Hesse says, "I think a less stubborn person would've given up! But I believed I could do it, and I had friends who were writers who believed I could do it, too. My stubbornness and their faith and encouragement of me kept me going through those nine years of rejection."[7]

Wish on a Unicorn

The idea for *Wish on a Unicorn* came from a battered and dirty stuffed unicorn that Hesse and her family found at a Vermont parking lot. The story's protagonist, Mags (short for Margaret), is in sixth grade. She has a younger sister and brother who feel to her like a burden. Her mother works at night, and Mags is responsible for taking care of Hannie, her mentally retarded sister. Her brother, Mooch, is too young to go to school. However, he's too smart and too bored to stay at home all day while their mother sleeps. Unfortunately, he has a talent for finding trouble—especially when he's hungry, which seems to be all the time.

Mags wants desperately to fit in with her classmates, but she, Hannie, and Mooch are bullied by the kids at school. When Hannie finds a dirty stuffed unicorn on the way home, she insists it has magical powers. Mags doesn't believe in the unicorn's powers, but there is so much she wants, and Hannie and Mooch's belief in the unicorn is so strong, that Mags starts believing, too.

As Hesse wrote *Wish on a Unicorn*, she recalled the tar paper shacks and the poverty of the families her father collected money from when she was a child. When it was published in 1991, *Wish on a Unicorn* was well received by critics who liked the way Hesse depicted a family that is rich in their feelings of love for each other but that doesn't have enough money to make ends meet. With the publication of *Wish on a Unicorn,* Hesse finally had the audience she had been working and preparing for, and nearly all of her books have been well received by critics and well loved by readers ever since.

5 Finding the Story

Hesse's second book, *Letters from Rifka*, is a story based on Hesse's family. She says, "When my grandparents died, I felt as if I had lost something I couldn't replace. I began asking my mother for stories about my grandparents. She didn't have them, but she suggested I ask my great-aunt Lucy. So I did. Lucy couldn't answer my questions about my grandparents either, but she could answer questions about herself. Her story is Rifka's story."[1]

Letters from Rifka would become the first of Hesse's historical novels, and it was an extensive undertaking in research. The story takes place in 1919. To write the book, Hesse needed to be well versed in the social and political conditions of that era. Because Rifka travels from eastern Europe to western Europe and eventually to the United States, Hesse also had to research the geography and history of these regions.

With *Rifka*, Hesse began the comprehensive approach to research that marks her as one of the leading writers of historical fiction for the young adult audience. She loves research and she loves libraries, and perhaps these two passions make her perfectly suited for the grand scale of the projects she takes on. She begins her research in the library's children's room, because writing for younger readers is often more simply organized and succinctly stated. From the bibliography of these books, she may also find other sources to read.

"My method is to saturate myself with the place, period, and people. I'm convinced it is impossible to be entirely accurate when writing historical fiction, but after reading so many sources, my ear begins to recognize the false notes, either in someone else's work or in my own. I cannot put full faith in the newspaper accounts, nor in the first person narratives. These help me to understand how it felt to live through the event, but I also need to take the long, historical, factually documented perspective into account while

I'm writing and revising. I often spend more time in the research stage (average nine months to a year) than the writing stage (average six months to nine months),"[2] Hesse says. "For *Rifka*, my research included reading historical collections (some engagingly written, some very dry), reading fiction written during and about the period, watching movies set in the period, and interviewing people who lived through or knew people who had lived through the period. After I'd filled my head with enough material, I felt prepared to begin writing."[3]

In *Letters from Rifka*, Rifka Nebrot is a twelve-year-old girl who is fleeing Russia with her family in the aftermath of World War I. In Russia, Jews are being persecuted. The family is escaping to seek a better life. They make their way to Poland, where they contract typhus and almost die. When they finally arrive in Warsaw, their family finds out that Rifka has ringworm. This means that even if Rifka makes the long voyage to the United States, the American officials will probably send her back to Europe. The Hebrew Immigrant Aid Society arranges for Rifka to travel to Belgium where she can recover. Her family goes on to America without her.

The story is told in the form of letters Rifka writes to her cousin in the margins of a book of poetry. When asked why she chose the format of the book as letters that are written but never sent, Hesse says that because Rifka is placed in so many difficult situations, she wanted her readers to know in advance that Rifka will survive the situation and live to write the next letter.

Letters from Rifka was Hesse's first big success as a young adult author. The book won numerous awards, two of which include a 1992 Sydney Taylor Book Award and a 1993 Christopher Medal. Another landmark came for Hesse when she appeared at a conference of the International Reading Association. Katherine Paterson, the writer whose book *Of Nightingales That Weep* was Hesse's very first inspiration to write young adult novels, was the keynote speaker. Hesse was finally able to tell her "unwitting mentor"[4] how much she had learned about writing by studying Katherine Paterson's books. Today, Hesse and Paterson are good friends.

The Writing Process of Karen Hesse

Even when she knows the subject of her book, before she can start writing, Hesse must first find the character who is best suited to tell the story. She says, "I think my work is very much character driven, very much the voice of the narrator, and that's how the process begins for me. I can hear the character speaking. I can hear the cadence of the voice and that voice draws the action, draws the plot to it. I don't know when I begin what age group I'm writing for. I don't know what's going to happen in the book."[5]

Thinking about her protagonist may happen in tandem with necessary research, if the story involves elements in which Hesse is not fluent. She loves research. The depth and extent of her dedication to this stage of the writing process is an important part of what distinguishes Hesse from other writers. "When I'm in the research stage of writing a book I'm like a person who is always hungry," she says. "I have stacks of books in my bedroom and my office and I eat them up. I often read more than one at a time because I am so eager to see what each has to say that I peek into one before I've finished with another. I don't pay as close attention to housekeeping, or preparing food for my family as I usually [do]. I am often up too late at night, finishing one more chapter, one more book, which leaves me grumpy and groggy the next morning. And then, as my head becomes more and more filled with data, I become the ultimate grump until I actually start writing. Once I start the writing process I relax and am able to get my family and my house back in order again."[6]

But once the writing begins, it preoccupies her in a different way. "I write very fast. When I'm writing on first draft, I'm just compulsive. It's hard for me to stop because I don't know how the book is going to end, and I'm a reader so I can't wait to find out. I write a very spare draft. It's done very quickly—usually in a matter of a week or two,"[7] she says. "I'll just write through the night, through the day, through the night, through the day, through the night, through the day, until I have the first draft. Once I have a very spare draft, maybe thirty to sixty pages long, I'll go back and read it and see what I've done because I haven't a clue. I haven't a clue what the book is about, why the book is about that, or what the character's motivation is, what the character needs. I simply listen to that voice coupled with the research in creating something."[8]

Once Hesse has finished her first draft, she takes some time away from the story, then dives in to begin revising and refining the story and the way she is telling it. Her process at this point becomes very precise. "I revise," she says. "I revise pages one through three one day, and then do pages two through five the next day, and then do three through six the next day, and four through seven the next day, so that it begins to grow very, very slowly. I'll go through a book that way until I get through to the end. That will be draft two. I just do that over and over again—probably seven to ten times—before I send it off to my editor for the first time."[9]

But before Hesse's work is ready to be seen by an editor, there are other eyes and other readers who help her to see the story from different angles and to best communicate what she wants to say. For many years, Hesse has been a member of a writer's group. The other members are Liza Ketchum, Eileen Christelow, Bob MacLean, and Wendy Watson. The members of this group present their writing and art (a few are book illustrators) to each other. They talk about what does and does not work in the projects that are being discussed. When Hesse feels her story is in good enough shape to benefit from the criticism of her peers, she submits it to the group.

Honing a book is complex labor for Hesse, in part because her versatility as a writer allows her to craft her work into many different shapes. "I don't start a book thinking I will write this as diary entries, or I will experiment with typeface and interior/exterior voice, or I will tell this story as a series of narrative poems. I simply try to tell the story the way the protagonist I've established would tell it. The way we speak, the way we dress, the way we walk, the way we act and react, all these subtle (and not so subtle) behaviors reflect who we are, what we think of ourselves, what our story is. Experimenting with narrative form is my attempt to marry shape with content; the physical appearance of character and story reflecting the essence of character and story."[10]

Hesse has written books as prose, poetry, letters, and diary entries. Because she continues to push the boundaries of storytelling for children and young adults, having colleagues and a family who have opinions and suggestions about her writing help to keep her moving forward. "When I finish writing a draft, the first reader is determined by the kind of book I'm trying to write," she says. "For example, my daughter Rachel understands me well; she also understands children's literature. If I am taking risks, if I am creating a sort of high-wire act with a story, I will give an early draft to Rachel to see if I'm making any sense at all. My writing group also gets an early look. They often see the manuscript two or three times during the years of revisions. My editor, of course, reads the manuscript at several stages in its development, and my husband and daughter Kate read the final drafts. If I need expert readers (and I often do), they read the manuscript in its earlier stages so that if I am heading down the wrong path they can correct me before I've invested too much time exploring a dead end."[11]

6 Inspiration Everywhere

In 1992, Hesse happened to catch the last half of a documentary on the Discovery Channel about the havoc that was wrought on a Ukrainian community after the nuclear plant at Chernobyl melted down. Before seeing the documentary, which was called *The Children of Chernobyl*, Hesse had not understood how truly devastating the accident had been. She says, "I was haunted by the images. I just sat there on the edge of my bed. I couldn't move. I watched it through to the end, and I tried to go to sleep, but the images were so firmly planted in my brain . . . I taped the program the next day and played it over fifteen to twenty times. I was totally obsessed. I couldn't let it go. Well, you know what writers do when they're obsessed with something—they write about it."[1]

Hesse's story about the aftermath of a nuclear power disaster is called *Phoenix Rising*. Hesse and her family live not far from a nuclear power plant called Vermont Yankee. Her obsession with *The Children of Chernobyl* film was fueled by the realization that her family, her life, and all that she knows would be endangered if there was an accident at the nuclear reactor. For this reason, she decided to set the story in her hometown of Brattleboro, Vermont. Originally, she set the story right at the center of the disaster, but that made the story too intense. After her agent suggested that she give up on the story, she put it away for a while. Still, it haunted her. The story wanted to be told and she wanted to tell it, but she could not find the right setting. An announcement in the local paper caught Hesse's attention and eventually solved the problem.

In her original version, Hesse had included a short scene that took place on a sheep farm. When she saw that a community nursery school was raising money by having an open house at a sheep farm, she decided to see what she might learn about sheep farming for her book. Once there, she realized that using the farm as the setting for the book would solve all of her story's problems. The owners of the farm became the sheep farm experts she relied upon to help her create a convincing portrayal of her characters' lives.

In her writing of *Phoenix Rising*, the impact of *Hiroshima*, the book Hesse read over and over as an twelve-year-old, is also evident. Her story uses the idea of simple, innocent people doing their best in the face of an immense tragedy. The book also deals with another problem in the lives of Hiroshima's survivors: the prejudices of those who were not affected against those who were.

Phoenix Rising

The nuclear disaster has already occurred when *Phoenix Rising*'s story begins. Boston has been destroyed, and all of New England has been affected. Thirteen-year-old Nyle and her grandmother live on a sheep farm in Vermont, and they are anxiously waiting to understand how seriously the fallout will affect them. They wear masks when they go outside to protect themselves from inhaling the radioactive fallout. They have radiation detectors to scan their home. Nyle and her grandmother have been lucky. They are still healthy, but some relatives have been badly hurt by the fallout. Nyle's best friend, Muncie, is sickly and small, and Muncie's parents are afraid for her health with so much radiation in the air. And then the Trents arrive.

Ezra Trent and his mother are evacuees from the heart of the accident. Both of them have been affected by the disaster, but Ezra, who is only a little older than Nyle, is near death. Nyle's grandmother has invited the Trents to live in the back bedroom of the house. Nyle thinks of this room as the "dying room" because both her mother and her grandfather spent their last, dying days there. Nyle doesn't want to make friends with the half-dead boy in the dying room, but eventually they do become friends and this friendship changes them both.

A Time of Angels

Hesse believes in angels. Having seen angels with her very own eyes as a child, she does not doubt the presence of angels at all. She says, "I think that this receptivity to mystical experience also welcomes the unconventional reality of fictional characters and worlds."[2] The fact that a series of small circumstances converged in Hesse's life to lead her to the story that became *A Time of Angels* may also suggest the hand of Hesse's own angels at work.

The idea for *A Time of Angels* came when Hesse asked a good friend who was about to undergo surgery if there was anything she might do to help. Her friend asked Hesse to simply "surround her with angels."[3] And Hesse did. Eager to help, Hesse wrote poems and stories that involved angels. When the surgery was a success, Hesse stopped thinking about angels and moved on to other projects. She forgot all about her angel file until her daughters found the angel stories on her computer and read them. They had one favorite story that they agreed should be turned into a book. Hesse didn't think much of the original idea, but when she sent it to her agent, her agent loved it. Then she sent it to an editor, and the editor loved it as well. Soon she was working on the story. The story as she had originally written it did not have a setting, but when Hesse saw a documentary about the influenza (the flu) epidemic of 1918 to 1919, she knew she had found a way to tell her angel story.

So again, Hesse went back to researching. She had to research the epidemic in order to devise the circumstances of her characters. In this case, she was lucky because there were still people who could talk firsthand about their experiences during the epidemic. Her interview subjects ranged in age from their seventies to nineties. Hesse used their stories in addition to the information she found through research.

The story of *A Time of Angels* begins in Boston, where Hannah Gold lives with her two younger sisters, her aunt Rose, and Rose's friend Vashti while the girls' parents are in Europe. Rose and Hannah's sisters fall ill with the flu. When Rose dies, Vashti sends Hannah to Albany, New York, to stay with a cousin of Rose's. On the train ride to Albany, Hannah becomes sick with the flu and she wakes up in Brattleboro, Vermont, where she is cared for by a stranger, Klaus Gerhard. Klaus is dealing with the bigotry of the community because he is a German immigrant at a time when the United States is at war against Germany. Because Hannah is Jewish, she might not have trusted Klaus if she knew his background. Klaus nurses Hannah back to health. Once she's healthy, she has to find her way back to her family. Throughout the story there is an angel who guards and comforts Hannah.

The Music of Dolphins

The idea for *The Music of Dolphins* has its roots in a radio program Hesse likes. She is a fan of *Fresh Air*, an interview program hosted by Terry Gross on National Public Radio. On *Fresh Air*, Hesse heard an interview with Russ Rymer, who had written a book called *Genie: A Scientific Tragedy*, about a young girl who had grown up with two abusive parents. Genie was kept strapped to a potty seat, and she was not allowed to make any noise at all. As a result, Genie never learned to speak, and she never learned how to live in human society. She was discovered accidentally on a rare occasion when her mother took her out of their home to submit an application at a government office. She was taken away from her family when social workers understood the conditions under which Genie had been forced to live. Cases like Genie's are rare. Feral children—children who are raised outside society and who don't know human language—offer scientists an opportunity to learn about language and the way humans learn language.

Unfortunately, because Genie did not learn fast enough or well enough, the scientists eventually stopped studying her and she was "thrown away"—given over to the government who placed her in a group home.

Hesse was fascinated by this story. She immediately read Russ Rymer's book about Genie and began to study feral children. Writing a story from the point of view of a feral child presented a bunch of problems. Ultimately, language—how we learn it, how we use it, and how language is connected to our emotional lives—is the subject of *The Music of Dolphins*. But before she could write the book, Hesse had to find a way to tell the story that would make sense to the reader and would make sense for Mila, the story's main character.

"You might think that I asked myself how can I choose the hardest task for myself as a writer?" Hesse says, "Mila is prelingual. She didn't have human language with which to convey human emotions, her thoughts, her needs, her desires, her fears. I needed a way to show that. It seems that the projects I choose demand a different way of telling than the regular prose narrative, but they are very satisfying when you get them right."[4] Because Genie's story ended so disastrously, Hesse wanted to find a way to create a feral character whose life might be able to have a better outcome.

The Music of Dolphins is set in the present day, but it was yet another story for which Hesse needed to do an immense amount of research. Because she chose to characterize Mila as a feral child who has been raised by a community of dolphins, she had to learn all she could about dolphins, everything she could about language, and everything she could about feral children. Then she had to figure out how likely or how possible it would be for a young child to grow and live in the ocean, eat the same diet as a dolphin's, and live without much exposure to fresh water. When she was able to sufficiently answer all of her questions and create a believable life for her character, her next challenge was to tell the story from Mila's point of view, using language as Mila acquired it.

The story of *The Music of Dolphins* begins when Mila is spotted by the Coast Guard and picked up. Initially, the Coast Guard assumes that she is an illegal alien who has swam to the island. But when they realize that she doesn't speak any human language but seems to speak dolphin, they understand that she is feral. The book details Mila's life as she is taught and studied by scientists. She does begin to communicate in English, but she is baffled by much of the behavior around her. The more time she spends learning the ways of humans, the more she longs for the life she had with the dolphins.

7 Poetry Returns

Hesse's Newbery Medal–award winning book, *Out of the Dust*, is historical fiction rich in its emotions, themes, and style. For Hesse, the story involved an eye-opening road trip and extensive research.

At one time, Hesse had an idea for a picture book about a girl in the city on a hot summer day. The girl wanted very badly for it to rain. The story was to be called *Come on, Rain!* Eventually, Hesse did write that book, but only after a few questions and a cross-country trip led her to write *Out of the Dust*. When Hesse first presented the idea to her writing group, Eileen Christelow, one of the group's members, asked why the girl wanted so much for it to rain. Hesse did not have an answer then, but as she reflected on Christelow's question, she thought back to a road trip to Colorado she had taken with another group member, Liza Ketchum.

In Hesse's Newbery acceptance speech for *Out of the Dust*, she recounted arriving in Kansas and experiencing a tornado for the first time. The quick changes in the weather and the colors of the land and sky surprised Hesse. She was deeply affected by seeing this different landscape. Although she did not write about it at the time, the images and the feeling of the trip stayed with her for three years before she used her experiences in *Out of the Dust*.

Eileen Christelow's question caused Hesse to begin to think of times in which people wanted desperately for it to rain. The Dust Bowl days, a period during America's Great Depression of the early 1930s, came to mind. During this period, in the Great Plains states, there was very little rain and crops failed. Many people gave up on farming as a result of the Dust Bowl. Many people from Oklahoma and neighboring states left their farms and headed west to California and other places they thought might offer a chance for a better life.

In order to re-create the mood and the history of those days, Hesse read many years' worth of back issues of the *Boise City News*. She also consulted the Oklahoma Historical Society. What's particularly remarkable about *Out of the Dust* is that after seventeen years of writing young adult novels (which was seventeen years of not being a poet), Hesse began writing poetry again. Now that her daughters were grown and she did not need to keep an ear out listening for them, she could hear the poetry. She heard the voice of Billie Jo Kelby, her protagonist in *Out of the Dust*, as free verse. The whole book is told through poetry from Billie Jo's perspective.

Out of the Dust

When *Out of the Dust* begins, Billie Jo Kelby lives with her parents on a farm. Her mother is expecting a new baby, and her father is trying to save the wheat in the face of a drought and to keep the dust from killing their crops. They are hoping for rain, and like their friends and neighbors, they are doing the best they can. Then, as the result of a terrible accident, Billie Jo's mother dies. Billie Jo is also hurt in the accident. She tells her story as she tries to heal her body, adjust to not having a mother, and grieves about the hard times that have fallen on her community.

Hesse has said that if she were writing *Out of the Dust* today, she would put "more hope in the earlier part of the book."[1] This may be so, but it is also clear that what interests Hesse most as she writes is the revelation of her characters' strengths in the face of adversity. "I never make up any of the bad things that happen to my characters," she says. "I love my characters too much to hurt them deliberately, even the prickly ones. It just so happens that in life, there's pain; sorrow lives in the shadow of joy, joy in the shadow of sorrow. The question is, do we let the pain reign triumphant, or do we find a way to grow, to transform, and ultimately transcend our pain?"[2]

Out of the Dust won the 1998 Newbery Medal, the highest prize given to children's authors. With the free verse poetry of the book, Hesse pioneered a new way of telling stories to young adults.

Since *Out of the Dust*, Hesse has published *Witness, Aleutian Sparrow* (2003), and *The Stone Lamp: Eight Stories of Hanukkah Through History*, three more books of historical fiction written in free verse. Even in books written as prose (*A Light in the Storm: The Civil War Diary of Amelia Martin* (1999) and *Stowaway* (1999), Hesse has continued to look back at history.

The Genius of Karen Hesse

In 2002, Hesse was chosen by the John D. and Catherine T. MacArthur Foundation for one of its "genius" fellowships. A sum of $500,000 is given by the foundation to people it feels have exhibited "extraordinary dedication in their creative pursuits." Hesse is only the second author of children's and young adult books to have earned such an honor.

Karen Hesse continues to write. "Often, our lives are so crowded, we need to hold to what is essential, and weed out what is not," she says. "Reading historical fiction gives us perspective. It gives us respite from the tempest of our present-day lives. It gives us a safe place in which we can grow, transform, transcend. It helps us understand, that sometimes the questions are too hard, that sometimes there are no answers, that sometimes there is only forgiveness."[3] In the service of learning and teaching these lessons, Hesse continues to discover hidden moments in history that she can excavate and enliven with her unique gifts. She is a keen observer and an ambitious storyteller. Indeed, few writers are better at climbing into the skin of a character to explain the world through the character's eyes. That is the genius of Karen Hesse.

"Young readers are asking for substance. They are asking for respect. They are asking for books that challenge, and confirm, and console," she says. "They are asking for us to listen to their questions and to help them find their own answers."[4] Karen Hesse is listening. She is trying to help.

Interview with Karen Hesse

NZINGHA CLARKE: What is the most rewarding part of being a writer for you?

KAREN HESSE: Perhaps the most rewarding part of being a writer is the freedom to explore . . . to explore the landscape of history, the landscape of humanity, to delve into human emotion, human motivation, to follow the threads of a story wherever those threads might lead. Every day is a day of discovery, every day promises adventure. No one drives me, pushes me, directs me. I drive myself, push myself to exhaustion, direct myself into unfamiliar territory. Even if a book never reaches completion at the end of a particular journey of exploration, it is still well worth the trip, it is the experience of being a writer, a hunter and gatherer, a farmer of words. It's pretty darn wonderful.

NZINGHA CLARKE: What is the most difficult part of the writing process for you?

KAREN HESSE: Finding the voice, finding the point of view. When you have the voice, you have the story. When you discover that unique point of view, the work goes like a racehorse. You simply have to hang on tight and relish the wind in your hair. But finding the voice, finding the point of view is sometimes like being in a dark room with a blindfold on. You grope and grope and it eludes you, and you despair and yet you grope some more. Sometimes I'll do months of research and after multiple attempts to find the story, I have to give up and abandon it. That is like a small death.

NZINGHA CLARKE: What advice do you have for a person who thinks that he or she wants to be a writer?

KAREN HESSE: Write! Keep a journal, a diary, write poetry, vignettes, short stories, character sketches, descriptions of places, people, things.

You don't have to think in terms of an entire book. Develop your powers of observation, use all of your senses, and don't forget to use your heart and soul as you take the measure of your world. Live life, experience a range of activities, be open to possibilities, look at the way things connect, intersect. Be a dedicated observer. And READ! Read every day. Read the paper, read magazines, read short stories, poetry, novels, nonfiction. Read fantasy and history and sports and biography. READ, READ, READ.

NZINGHA CLARKE: Who, among all the characters in your books, do you most closely identify with? Why?

KAREN HESSE: Hmmm. That's such a difficult question to answer. Until I wrote *Witness*, I thought Hannah, from *A Time of Angels*, most closely matched me in personality. But I'd have to say Leanora [from *Witness*] and I have even more in common. It would be interesting to look at the characters of Hannah and Leanora, note their similarities. I suspect that would give you a very accurate window into who I am.

NZINGHA CLARKE: In the previous chapters, we learned of the impact of John Hersey's *Hiroshima* on you as a young adult and how the work of Katherine Paterson first inspired you to become a young adult novelist. Whose work is presently inspiring you? Why?

KAREN HESSE: I'm fascinated by the work of David Almond. I love his rich prose style and his otherworldly sense of being in the universe. I'm also dazzled by Paul Fleischman's body of work which I find innovative, egoless, and stunning. I am first and foremost a reader and when I discover a book with a strong narrative voice and a striking prose style, I gladly surrender my heart to it. Individual titles take me hostage every year and I willingly live inside them from the first page until well beyond the last.

NZINGHA CLARKE: It's often said that young people today are less interested in reading and are less literate than their counterparts in earlier generations. Do you agree or disagree? How does this affect your work as a writer, if at all?

KAREN HESSE: I'm certainly not an authority on the literacy levels of young people today as compared to their counterparts in earlier generations. My mail indicates there are thousands and thousands of dedicated young readers, thoughtful individuals who willingly seek out books. These readers offer insight, depth of understanding, compassionate response to what they've read, responses that fill me with awe and wonder. I write for them and I hope I never, never disappoint them.

NZINGHA CLARKE: Do you feel that life for young people today is more or less challenging than it was for you at the same age? Why?

KAREN HESSE: Again, I am not an expert on the challenges of contemporary youth compared to the challenges I met as a child. The world is certainly a different place than it was when I was growing up. There were pockets of horror then just as there are pockets of horror now. But there were also deep pools of beauty, generosity, kindness. Those pools exist today, too.

NZINGHA CLARKE: Do you think young readers should be guided as to what they read, or is it better simply to encourage them to read whatever interests them?

KAREN HESSE: Young readers should never be discouraged from reading what interests them, but

sometimes you don't know what you'll find interesting until someone introduces you to it. Imagine
if you'd never tasted chocolate pudding . . . if you'd
only always eaten pie. Well, to look at it, chocolate
pudding doesn't have much to commend it. It's
kind of muddy, not quite solid, nor quite liquid.
Ah, but one taste and your eyes light up. Bingo,
you've found something new to love. It can be like
that with books, too.

NZINGHA CLARKE: Does literature (for young
people or for anyone else) need to have a message?
Does that message ultimately need to be positive?

KAREN HESSE: Good grief. My answer to both
of these questions is NO! In fact, I would say it's
imperative that literature not have a "message."
We don't want to tell readers what to think! We
simply want them to think. As for happy endings
(my interpretation of "positive"), young readers
know that not all endings are happy. They want to
be entertained, but they also want us to be honest
with them. We owe that to them.

NZINGHA CLARKE: What answer would you
give to a young person who asks, "Why should
I read?"

KAREN HESSE: Phew! Do you have a couple of days to discuss this question? In a nutshell, this world is a complicated, unpredictable place. The world inside a book places order on chaos. It invites the reader in for a respite from their own complications. It gives readers a chance to walk awhile in someone else's shoes, to explore the world of the other with an intimacy seldom permitted in the real world. The insight that particular opportunity affords is priceless. Books contain knowledge, laughter, thrills, adventures, sorrow, love, hate, the entire range of life, of human emotion, but packaged between two cardboard covers. Reading is an escape into yourself, into the you that is part of the universal stream of life. Reading is one of the extraordinary miracles of humanity.

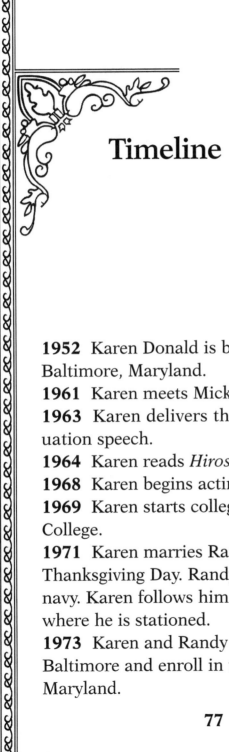

Timeline

1952 Karen Donald is born on August 29 in Baltimore, Maryland.

1961 Karen meets Mickey Czarney.

1963 Karen delivers the sixth-grade graduation speech.

1964 Karen reads *Hiroshima* by John Hersey.

1968 Karen begins acting.

1969 Karen starts college at Towson State College.

1971 Karen marries Randy Hesse on Thanksgiving Day. Randy is enlisted in the navy. Karen follows him to Norfolk, Virginia, where he is stationed.

1973 Karen and Randy Hesse return to Baltimore and enroll in the University of Maryland.

1975 Karen graduates from the University of Maryland.

1976 Randy Hesse graduates from the University of Maryland. The Hesses pack their truck and travel around the United States for six months. Their journey ends in Brattleboro, Vermont.

1978 Karen stops writing poetry. Karen Hesse discovers Katherine Peterson's book *Of Nightingales That Weep* and decides to write children's books.

April 1979 Karen's daughter Kate is born.

May 1982 Karen's daughter Rachel is born.

1991 Holt publishes *Wish on a Unicorn.*

1992 Holt publishes *Letters from Rifka.*

1993 Holt publishes *Lavender.* MacMillan publishes *Poppy's Chair.* Crown publishes *Lester's Dog.*

1994 Holt publishes *Phoenix Rising* and *Sable.*

1995 Hyperion publishes *A Time of Angels.*

1996 Scholastic publishes *The Music of Dolphins.* After seventeen years, Karen Hesse returns to poetry and writes *Out of the Dust.*

1997 Scholastic publishes *Out of the Dust.*

1998 Scholastic publishes *Just Juice* and *Come On, Rain!*

1999 Scholastic publishes *A Light in the Storm: The Civil War Diary of Amelia Martin.* Margaret K. Elderry Books publishes *Stowaway.*

2001 Scholastic publishes *Witness*.

2002 Karen Hesse is chosen for a MacArthur "genius" award.

2003 Hyperion publishes *The Stone Lamp: Eight Stories of Hanukkah Through History*. Margaret K. Elderry Books publishes *Aleutian Sparrow*.

2004 Scholastic publishes *The Cats in Kransinski Square*.

Selected
Reviews from
School Library
Journal

Aleutian Sparrow
2003

Gr 6 Up—In June, 1942, Japanese forces attacked the Aleutian Islands. Within days of the attack, the U.S. military removed the Native people of these islands to relocation centers in Alaska's southwest, supposedly for their own protection. Conditions in these camps were deplorable. The Aleuts were held for approximately three years, and many of them died. In a series of short, unrhymed verses, Hesse tells this moving story through the eyes and voice of a girl of Aleut and Caucasian heritage. The novel begins at a happy time for Vera, in May, 1942, and ends with her return home in April, 1945. During the course of the story, readers see all that the Aleut people endure during these years—bewilderment, prejudice, despair, illness, death, and everyday living that does include moments of humor and even a budding romance for Vera. Hesse's verses are short and flow seamlessly, one into another. Her use of similes is a powerful tool in describing people, scenes, events, and emotions. Some less sophisticated readers, however, may not catch the nuances of phrases such as, "-where blossoms framed the steaming pools like masses of perfumed hair" or "-where the old ways steep like tea in a cup of hours." Ending on a hopeful note, Aleutian Sparrow brings to light an important time in American history, and in the process introduces readers to Aleut culture.

Letters from Rifka
1992

Gr 4–7—Refused passage in 1919 because she has ringworm, a young Jewish girl from Russia battles supercilious officials and yards of red tape before she is finally reunited with her family in America. Historical fiction with a memorable heroine, a vivid sense of place, and a happily-ever-after ending.

The Music of Dolphins
1996

Gr 6–9—After a plane crash off the coast of Cuba, a four-year-old survives, nurtured by dolphins. At adolescence, the girl is "rescued" by the Coast Guard and turned over to a scientist who has a government grant to study the part language acquisition plays in socialization. Mila, the other-worldly "dolphin girl," is enthusiastic to please, learning to speak words and write her thoughts on a computer, but gradually she understands that she is a prisoner "in the net of humans." She begins to lose ground, regressing physically, begging to be returned to the sea. Hesse's skill is in making readers believe in this wise, intuitive feral child. Mila's longing for the sea and her dolphin family is so achingly palpable that her return is equally believable. Her story is told in her own perfectly sustained voice: the clear and simple, but profound and poetic language of a "foreigner" with a keen mind and resonant spirit but limited vocabulary. Readers, engrossed, will follow the intriguing device of changing typeface that indicates Mila's evolution-flowing script, to chunky bold, to standard size, and back-reflecting changes within her character. Deceptively easy in format, this is a complex and demanding book. Evoking a Selkie myth, it is a reminder that the link between humankind and nature is mysterious and ignored at our peril. This powerful exploration of how we become human and how the soul endures is a song of beauty and sorrow, haunting and unforgettable.

Out of the Dust
1997

Gr 5 Up—After facing loss after loss during the Oklahoma Dust Bowl, Billie Jo begins to reconstruct her life. A triumphant story, eloquently told through prose-poetry.

Phoenix Rising
1994

Gr 6–9—A Vermont sheep farm seems an unlikely place to worry about radiation and its effects. However, Nyle Sumner, 13, and her grandmother are completely surrounded by the grotesque results of an accident at a nuclear-power plant. Because of the accident, Nyle's cousin Bethany has radiation poisoning. Then Gran does the unthinkable: she takes in two fugitives who were exposed to the worst of the radiation, Miriam Trent and her son, Ezra, who is also sick with the poisoning. They stay in the back bedroom, the room marked by the death of Nyle's mother and grandfather. Now it seems likely that it will be the place that Ezra dies too. The bleak setting of this

book serves as a backdrop for the sensitive inter-
action among the main characters. Gran quietly
acts on her principles, Nyle overcomes her own
feelings to help Ezra, and her best friend, Muncie,
forgives past wrongs for the sake of friendship.
The characters overcome adversity, not through
heroic deeds of epic proportions, but through
simple acts of kindness. The message is poignant,
but not overpowering. Hesse has displayed con-
siderable skill in creating a contemporary tale of
hope and love rising, like a phoenix, from destruc-
tion and despair.

Stowaway
1999

Gr 5–9—The protagonist of this spirited 18th-
century sea story is 11-year-old Nicholas Young, an
English butcher's apprentice who flees his abusive
master and bribes his way aboard His Majesty's
Bark Endeavour. Captain James Cook pilots the
vessel to parts of the South Pacific still uncharted
by Europeans. With the help of a few compassionate sailors, the boy remains hidden for four
anguishing weeks and emerges only when assured
that the ship is too far out to sea to return him
home to Plymouth. For three years, Nicholas has
adventures beyond his imagination and faithfully

records his impressions. His journal brims with the beauty and power of the sea, the lure of undiscovered lands, and the friendship and mentoring from great men like Cook and naturalist Joseph Banks, who catalogues the marine and plant life along the way. The lad also describes the hardships and cruelties to which he is witness, such as floggings, disease, and death; savages and cannibals; and devastating storms. Hesse is a master storyteller who gives Nicholas an authentic voice, often using archaic phrasings and spellings to flavor his narrative. Ultimately, his voyage is one of self-discovery, as the boy tries to prove his mettle with a much older, more seasoned crew, often confronting his own mortality in the process. The author's subtle yet thorough attention to detail creates a memorable tale that is a virtual encyclopedia of life in the days when England ruled the seas.

A Time of Angels
1995

Gr 6–9—A warm, personal novel set in Boston during 1918. Hannah Gold, 14, and her two sisters live with their Tanta Rose while their parents are trapped in Russia because of the war. Although life is not easy, Tanta Rose provides for the girls as best she can. Rose's companion Vashti, however, feels that the girls are an intrusion. When the deadly influenza epidemic ravishes the city, Hannah's world is turned upside-down. Driven away by Vashti after Rose's death, the feverish young woman is guided to safety by a beautiful, ethereal girl (actually, an angel) who saved her life once before. She is nursed back to health on a Vermont farm by an old man whose strength and wisdom give her the courage to go back to Boston and to make peace with Vashti. Aspects of Jewish culture are nicely incorporated into the story, as are period details. However, some plot elements may cause confusion. The angel, portrayed as a guiding force instead of a fully developed character, interacts with Hannah on an almost subconscious level. Also, some of Hannah's actions do not seem realistic. Shortcomings aside, Hesse offers readers much to enjoy, analyze, and consider in this piece of historical fiction with a mystical bent.

Wish on a Unicorn
1991

Gr 4–6—Margaret Wade's family lives on the edge of poverty. Her mother is a single parent who works at night, and Mags feels beset by responsibilities and worries far beyond those of other 12-year-olds. Hannie, her retarded half-sister, finds a stuffed unicorn and is sure that it can grant wishes; Mags, too, almost comes to believe in the toy's power. There is no magic, but the events the unicorn's discovery precipitates lead Mags to a new realization of the depth of her love for her family. Hesse is sensitive to the youngster's mixed feelings of duty, caring, and frustration. Her plot moves satisfactorily, and she is successful in depicting the family's everyday environment; her description of the dinner Mags fixes for her brother and sister speaks volumes. The narrative is not always smooth, and the overuse of similes is distracting, but Hesse does capture the spirits of a stalwart young heroine and her family.

Witness
2001

Gr 6 Up—In this remarkable and powerful book, Hesse invites readers to bear witness to the Ku Klux Klan's activities in a small Vermont town in the 1920s. Using free verse as she did in *Out of the Dust* (Scholastic, 1997), the narrative here is expanded to encompass the voices of 11 towns-people, young and old, of various races and creeds. The story is divided into five acts, and would lend itself beautifully to performance. The plot unfolds smoothly, and the author creates multidimensional characters, all of whom seem very real. One of the least sympathetic is an 18-year-old boy who begins the book by wanting to open a classroom window to let out the smell of the black girl. By the end, he is transformed by circumstances in a thoroughly plausible way. The writing includes vivid images, such as when Leanora, the black girl, sees a burning cross. She hides in a closet: "in that dark and narrow place,/ i opened a hole for myself/ but no matter how i turned,/ the light from the cross/ curled its bright claws under the door." It also includes some quiet yet irreducible moments that resonate long after the book is put down. The small details seem just right, and demonstrate that this is much more than a social tract. It's a thoughtful look at people and their capacity for love and hate.

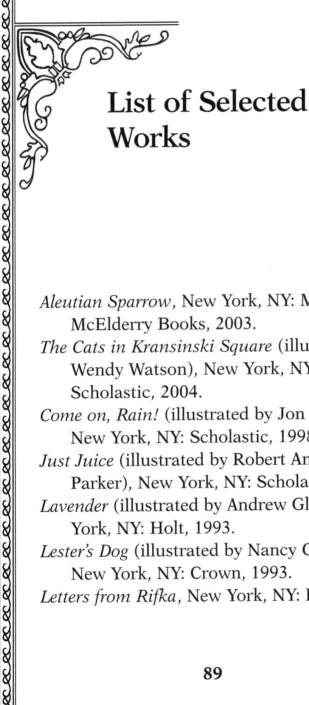

List of Selected Works

Aleutian Sparrow, New York, NY: Margaret K. McElderry Books, 2003.

The Cats in Kransinski Square (illustrated by Wendy Watson), New York, NY: Scholastic, 2004.

Come on, Rain! (illustrated by Jon J. Muth), New York, NY: Scholastic, 1998.

Just Juice (illustrated by Robert Andrew Parker), New York, NY: Scholastic, 1998.

Lavender (illustrated by Andrew Glass), New York, NY: Holt, 1993.

Lester's Dog (illustrated by Nancy Carpenter), New York, NY: Crown, 1993.

Letters from Rifka, New York, NY: Holt, 1992.

A Light in the Storm: The Civil War Diary of Amelia Martin, New York, NY: Scholastic, 1999.

The Music of Dolphins, New York, NY: Scholastic, 1996.

Out of the Dust, New York, NY: Scholastic, 1997.

Phoenix Rising, New York, NY: Holt, 1994.

Poppy's Chair (illustrated by Kay Life), New York, NY: Macmillan, 1993.

Sable (illustrated by Marcia Sewall), New York, NY: Holt, 1994.

The Stone Lamp: Eight Stories of Hanukkah Through History (illustrations by Brian Pinkney), New York, NY: Hyperion, 2003.

Stowaway (illustrations by Robert Andrew Parker), New York, NY: Margaret K. McElderry Books, 1999.

A Time of Angels, New York, NY: Hyperion, 1995.

Wish on a Unicorn, New York, NY: Holt, 1991.

Witness, New York, NY: Scholastic, 2001.

List of Selected Awards

Letters from Rifka **(1992)**
The Christopher Awards Books for Young
   People, 1993 (The Christopher Medal)
International Reading Association Children's
   Book Award, 1993
The Sydney Taylor Book Awards, 1992

A Light in the Storm: The Civil War Diary of
Amelia Martin **(1999)**
Maryland Children's Book Award, 2002

The Music of Dolphins **(1996)**
The Golden Kite Award Honor Book, 1996

Out of the Dust (1997)

Newbery Medal, 1998
Scott O'Dell Award for Historical Fiction, 1998

Phoenix Rising (1994)

American Library Association (ALA) Best Books
  for Young Adults, 1995
Arizona Young Readers' Award, 1998
New York Charlotte Award, 1998
South Carolina Children's Book Award, 1997

A Time of Angels (1995)

International Reading Association Teachers'
  Choices, 1996
International Reading Association Young Adults'
  Choices, 1997

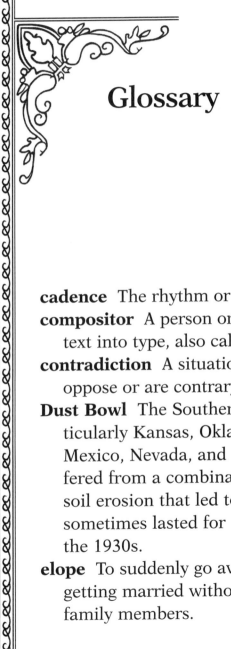

Glossary

cadence The rhythm or inflection of sound.

compositor A person or a company that sets text into type, also called a typesetter.

contradiction A situation in which elements oppose or are contrary to each other.

Dust Bowl The Southern Plains states (particularly Kansas, Oklahoma, Texas, New Mexico, Nevada, and Arkansas) that suffered from a combination of drought and soil erosion that led to dust storms and sometimes lasted for days at a time during the 1930s.

elope To suddenly go away for the purpose of getting married without the knowledge of family members.

expert reader A person possessing specific skills or knowledge on a subject who reviews a manuscript to make sure that its content on the subject is accurate and realistic.

forthright Direct or straightforward.

freelance An independent worker who is not on salary, but is employed only when he or she is needed.

group home A home in which children who are not being taken care of by their families are raised by a professional team of adults.

guise Manner of outward appearance.

hospice A program that provides care for the terminally ill.

in tandem Together; two or more parts coming together to work together.

integrity A person's firm code of morals and values; wholeness or uprightness.

open house An event in which a person or a group entertains a large group by general invitation.

prelingual Relating to a stage before language is acquired.

proofreader A person who marks and corrects written work.

reckoning Understanding and accepting the truth about something.

respite A short period of rest.

ringworm A group of contagious fungal diseases that causes scaly ring-shaped patches on the skin.

subterranean Beneath the earth; under the surface.

succinctly Expressed clearly and precisely with no wasted words.

tempest A violent storm.

tragedy A disastrous or unfortunate event.

typesetter A person who sets written material into type.

typhus A group of bacterial diseases that can be spread to humans by fleas and body lice. Symptoms include high fever, headaches, and rash.

unwitting Unaware.

For More Information

Due to the changing nature of Internet links, the Rosen Publishing Group, Inc., has developed an online list of Web sites related to the subject of this book. This site is updated regularly. Please use this link to access the list:

http://www.rosenlinks.com/lab/kahe

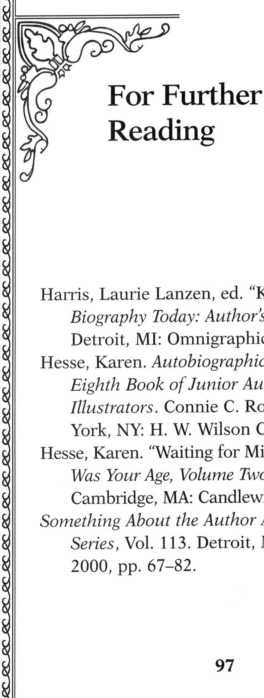

For Further Reading

Harris, Laurie Lanzen, ed. "Karen Hesse." *Biography Today: Author's Series*, Vol. 5. Detroit, MI: Omnigraphics, Inc., 1999.

Hesse, Karen. *Autobiographical Statement. Eighth Book of Junior Authors and Illustrators*. Connie C. Rockman, ed. New York, NY: H. W. Wilson Company, 2000.

Hesse, Karen. "Waiting for Midnight." *When I Was Your Age, Volume Two*. Amy Ehrlich, ed. Cambridge, MA: Candlewick Press, 1999.

Something About the Author Autobiography Series, Vol. 113. Detroit, MI: Gale Group, 2000, pp. 67–82.

Bibliography

Authors and Artists for Young Adults,
    Vol. 52. "Karen Hesse." Detroit, MI: Gale
    Group, 2003.
Beck, Cathy, Linda Gwyn, Dick Koblitz, Anne
    O'Connor, Kathryn Mitchell Pierce, and
    Susan Wolf. "Talking About Books: Karen
    Hesse." *Language Arts*, January 1999,
    pp. 263–271.
Bowen, Brenda. "Karen Hesse." *Horn Book
    Magazine*, July–August 1998, pp. 428–432.
Bryant, Ellen. "Honoring the Complexities of
    Our Lives: An Interview with Karen
    Hesse." *Voices from the Middle*, April 1997,
    pp. 38–49.

BWI Books. "An Interview with Karen Hesse." Retrieved July 6, 2004 (http://www.bwibooks. com/khesse.html).

Casey, Carol. "Carried by Creative Currents." Retrieved July 6, 2004 (http://www.childrenslit. com/f_hesse.html).

Devereaux, Elizabeth. "Karen Hesse: A Poetics of Perfectionism." *Publishers Weekly*, February 8, 1999, pp. 190–191.

Harris, Laurie Lanzen, ed. "Karen Hesse." Biography Today: *Author's Series*, Vol. 5. Detroit, MI: Omnigraphics, Inc., 1999.

Hendershot, Judy, and Jackie Peck. "Newbery Medal Winner Karen Hesse Brings Billie Jo's Voice Out of the Dust." *Reading Teacher*, May 1999, pp. 856–858.

Hesse, Karen. *Autobiographical Statement. Eighth Book of Junior Authors and Illustrators*. Connie C. Rockman, ed. New York, NY: H. W. Wilson Company, 2000.

Hesse, Karen. "Letter to Audrey Conant, Information Skills Committee, June 12, 1993." *Maine Association of School Libraries. Maine Sampler Part III*. Retrieved August 21, 2004 (http://www.maslibraries.org/infolit/ samplers/rifka.html).

Hesse, Karen. Karen Hesse Interview Transcript
(interviewed by Scholastic students).
Retrieved August 21, 2004 (http://www2.
scholastic.com/teachers/authorsandbooks/
authorstudies/authorhome.jhtml?authorID=
45&collateralID=5338&displayName=
Interview+Transcript&displayName=
Interview%20Transcript).

Hesse, Karen "1998 Newbery Speech for *Out
of the Dust.*" Delivered June 27, 1998.
Scholastic. Retrieved July 6, 2004 (http://
www.scholastic.com/titles/outofthedust/
speech.htm).

Hesse, Karen. "Thank You Mr. Ball." *Instructor*,
January–February 1999, p. 86.

Hesse, Karen. "Waiting for Midnight." *When I
Was Your Age, Volume Two*. Amy Ehrlich, ed.
Cambridge, MA: Candlewick Press, 1999.

Jones, Mary Varilla. "A Reading Guide to Out of
the Dust." *Scholastic Book Files*, New York,
NY: Scholastic: 2004, pp. 11–16.

O'Malley, Judy. "Talking with . . . Karen Hesse."
Book Links, September 1999, pp. 54–61.

Shawnee News-Star. "Newbery Winner Adds
Somber Voice to Revised Summer Reading
Lists." June 30, 1998. Retrieved August 21,
2004 (http://www.news-star.com/stories/
063098/art-newbery.html).

Stover, Lois T. "Karen Hesse." *Writers for Young Adults*. Ted Hipple, ed. Woodbridge, CT: Charles Scribner's Sons, 2000.

Something About the Author Autobiography Series, Vol. 113. Detroit, MI: Gale Group, 2000, pp. 67–82.

Source Notes

Introduction

1. Karen Hesse. Karen Hesse Interview Transcript (interviewed by Scholastic students). Retrieved August 21, 2004 (http://www2.scholastic.com/ teachers/authorsandbooks/authorstudies/ authorhome.jhtml?authorID=45&collateralID= 5338&displayName=Interview+Transcript& displayName=Interview%20Transcript).

2. BWI Books, "An Interview with Karen Hesse." Retrieved July 6, 2004 (http://www.bwibooks. com/khesse.html).

3. Lois T. Stover, "Karen Hesse." *Writers for Young Adults*. Ted Hipple, ed. (Woodbridge, CT: Charles Scribner's Sons, 2000).

4. Elizabeth Devereaux, "Karen Hesse: A Poetics of Perfectionism." *Publishers Weekly*, February 8, 1999, p. 190.

5. Carol Casey, "Carried By Creative Currents." Retrieved July 6, 2004 (http://www.childrenslit. com/f_hesse.html). Originally appeared in *Terp*, University of Maryland alumni magazine, Winter 2004, pp. 104, 107.
6. Brenda Bowen, "Karen Hesse." *Horn Book Magazine*, July–August 1998, p. 429.

Chapter 1

1. *Something About the Author Autobiography Series*, Vol. 113 (Detroit, MI: Gale Group, 2000), p. 70.
2. Ibid, p. 71.
3. Karen Hesse, *Autobiographical Statement. Eighth Book of Junior Authors and Illustrators*. Connie C. Rockman, ed. (New York, NY: H. W. Wilson Company, 2000).
4. Judy O'Malley, "Talking with . . . Karen Hesse." *Book Links*, September 1999, p. 56.
5. Ellen Bryant, "Honoring the Complexities of Our Lives: An Interview with Karen Hesse." *Voices from the Middle*, April 1997, p. 41.
6. Karen Hesse. Karen Hesse Interview Transcript (interviewed by Scholastic students). Retrieved August 21, 2004 (http://www2.scholastic.com/ teachers/authorsandbooks/authorstudies/ authorhome.jhtml?authorID=45&collateralID= 5338&displayName=Interview+Transcript& displayName=Interview%20Transcript).

7. Judy Hendershot, and Jackie Peck, "Newbery Medal Winner Karen Hesse Brings Billie Jo's Voice Out of the Dust." *Reading Teacher*, May 1999, p. 856.

8. Bryant, p. 42.

9. Ibid.

Chapter 2

1. Cathy Beck, Linda Gwyn, Dick Koblitz, Anne O'Connor, Kathryn Mitchell Pierce, and Susan Wolf, "Talking About Books: Karen Hesse." *Language Arts*, January 1999 [referencing a May 1998 interview by Dick Koblitz], p. 263.

2. BWI Books, "An Interview with Karen Hesse." Retrieved July 6, 2004 (http://www.bwibooks.com/khesse.html).

Chapter 3

1. *Something About the Author Autobiography Series*, Vol. 113. (Detroit, MI: Gale Group, 2000), p. 81.

2. Carol Casey, "Carried by Creative Currents." Retrieved July 6, 2004 (http://www.childrenslit.com/f_hesse.html). Originally appeared in *Terp*, University of Maryland alumni magazine, Winter 2004 issue, pp. 104, 107.

3. Ibid.

Chapter 4

1. Elizabeth Devereaux, "Karen Hesse: A Poetics of Perfectionism." *Publishers Weekly*, February 8, 1999, p. 190.

2. Ellen Bryant, "Honoring the Complexities of Our Lives: An Interview with Karen Hesse." *Voices from the Middle*, April 1997, p. 42.

3. Cathy Beck, Linda Gwyn, Dick Koblitz, Anne O'Connor, Kathryn Mitchell Pierce, and Susan Wolf, "Talking About Books: Karen Hesse." *Language Arts*, January 1999, p. 263.

4. Devereaux, p. 190.

5. *Shawnee News-Star*, "Newbery Winner Adds Somber Voice to Revised Summer Reading Lists." June 30, 1998. Retrieved August 21, 2004 (http://www.news-star.com/stories/063098/art-newbery.html).

6. Devereaux, p. 190.

7. *Authors and Artists for Young Adults*, Vol. 52. "Karen Hesse" (Detroit, MI: Gale Group, 2003).

Chapter 5

1. Karen Hesse. Karen Hesse Interview Transcript (interviewed by Scholastic students). Retrieved August 21, 2004 (http://www2.scholastic.com/teachers/authorsandbooks/authorstudies/authorhome.jhtml?authorID=45&collateralID=5338&displayName=Interview+Transcript&displayName=Interview%20Transcript).

2. BWI Books, "An Interview with Karen Hesse." Retrieved July 6, 2004 (http://www.bwibooks.com/khesse.html).

3. Karen Hesse, "Letter to Audrey Conant, Information Skills Committee, June 12, 1993." Maine Association of School Libraries. *Maine*

Sampler Part III. Retrieved August 21, 2004 (http://www.maslibraries.org/infolit/samplers/rifka.html).

4. Lois T. Stover, "Karen Hesse." *Writers for Young Adults*. Ted Hipple, ed. Woodbridge, CT: Charles Scribner's Sons, 2000.

5. Cathy Beck, Linda Gwyn, Dick Koblitz, Anne O'Connor, Kathryn Mitchell Pierce, and Susan Wolf, "Talking About Books: Karen Hesse." *Language Arts*, January 1999, p. 264.

6. Hesse, "Letter to Audrey Conant, Information Skills Committee, June 12, 1993."

7. Ellen Bryant, "Honoring the Complexities of Our Lives: An Interview with Karen Hesse." *Voices from the Middle*, April 1997, p. 42.

8. Cathy Beck, Linda Gwyn, Dick Koblitz, Anne O'Connor, Kathryn Mitchell Pierce, and Susan Wolf, "Talking about Books: Karen Hesse." *Language Arts*, January 1999, p. 264.

9. Bryant, pp. 42–43.

10. Judy O'Malley. "Talking with . . . Karen Hesse." *Book Links*, September 1999, p. 55.

11. Mary Varilla Jones, "A Reading Guide to Out of the Dust." (New York, NY: Scholastic Book Files, 2004), p. 13.

Chapter 6

1. Ellen Bryant, "Honoring the Complexities of Our Lives: An Interview with Karen Hesse." *Voices from the Middle*, April 1997, pp. 39–40.

2. Carol Casey, "Carried by Creative Currents." Retrieved July 6, 2004 (http://www.childrenslit. com/f_hesse.html). Originally appeared in *Terp*, University of Maryland alumni magazine, Winter 2004 issue, pp. 103, 104.
3. Bryant, p. 41.
4. Judy Hendershot, and Jackie Peck, "Newbery Medal Winner Karen Hesse Brings Billie Jo's Voice Out of the Dust." *Reading Teacher*, May 1999, p. 858.

Chapter 7

1. Karen Hesse. Karen Hesse Interview Transcript (interviewed by Scholastic students). Retrieved August 21, 2004 (http://www2.scholastic.com/ teachers/authorsandbooks/authorstudies/ authorhome.jhtml?authorID=45&collateralID= 5338&displayName=Interview+Transcript& display Name=Interview%20Transcript).
2. Karen Hesse, "1998 Newbery Speech for *Out of the Dust*." Retrieved June 27, 1998. Scholastic.com. Retrieved July 6, 2004 (http://www.scholastic.com/ titles/outofthedust/speech.htm).
3. Ibid.
4. Ibid.

Index

About the Author

While Nzingha Clarke was researching the life of Karen Hesse, she realized her path was similar to Hesse's in several ways. Like Hesse, she began writing as a child. Clarke is also drawn to challenging subject matter and characters whose stories are not often told. Clarke has also worked as a proofreader and copy editor while on her way to becoming a published author of short stories. Born in New York City, she now lives in Los Angeles.

Photo Credits

Cover, p.2 © AP/Wide World Photos.

Designer: Tahara Anderson
Editor: Leigh Ann Cobb
Photo Researcher: Hillary Arnold